# Born to be Wild
# Little Foxes

Ariane Chottin

Words that appear in the glossary are printed in
**boldface** type the first time they occur in the text.

**GARETHSTEVENS**
**GS**
PUBLISHING
A WRC Media Company

# Little Mischief-Makers

Little foxes play often with their brothers and sisters. Their play is very physical and lively. They will play-fight by twos or threes or all at the same time. Sneaking up on each other, they move slowly and quietly. Using their four paws and short legs, they leap straight up, then roll around with each other like balls of fur. The little foxes' days of fun help increase their physical strength and sharpen their attentiveness.

**Each little fox has a round stomach, small ears, and a short, pointed tail. When they play, little foxes nip each other and use their jaws to hold on tightly.**

## What do you think?

Why do little foxes play close to their dens?

**a)** to have shelter in case of danger

**b)** because they are not curious about the outside world

**c)** because they are afraid of bright sunshine

3

Four weeks after they are born, little foxes, which are called pups, **venture** out onto the paths that are near their dens, or homes. They are careful not to wander too far. During the day, pups play nearby for about an hour before going inside again. The tiniest noise or fear will send them running back to the den. The pups' mothers teach them to stay safe in their family shelters.

**Their playtime activities give pups the training they will need to defend their territories as adults. While pups are still very small, they already make threatening, growling sounds.**

**At four weeks of age, little foxes have blue eyes that seem a little off center. Soon, the pupils of their eyes will turn gold and oval in shape, like their parents' eyes.**

4

When little foxes get tired, from eating well and playing hard, they fall on top of each other in a pile. Then, little by little, they each find a comfortable sleeping position.

# Hunting Tricks

Two months after birth, a little fox has grown and changed. Its paws, ears, and tail are longer, and the pup is now ready to learn to hunt. Like its parents, a pup eats a wide variety of foods. It hunts rabbits, mice, **moles**, and **shrews** and also eats some kinds of fruits. When a fox pup becomes a good hunter, it will be able to catch birds, too.

## What do you think?

How does a little fox hunt for its prey?

**a)** like a cat

**b)** like a dog

**c)** like a wolf

By the time a fox pup learns to hunt, it has already tasted live **prey** many times. The fox's mother, or sometimes its father, brings prey back to the den and drops it in front of the pups.

**A little fox hunts for its prey like a cat.**

A fox pup learns to hunt by watching its mother and by playing with the live prey she brings to her young.

A fox hunts the same way a cat does. It moves forward silently — carefully lifting its paws, ears pointed toward the prey — then pounces to land on its prey! This **solitary** hunter is a very good runner, too. It can outrun a rabbit by chasing it for a long time, until the rabbit is tired.

When a fox spots a small rodent, it flattens itself on the ground, then leaps up to catch the prey. Next, the fox seems to do a kind of dance, playing with its prey just like a cat plays with a mouse.

8

A fox is not a
big eater.  One
small animal
is enough food
for several
days.  When a
fox has eaten
enough, it
buries any
extra food so
that it has a
reserve supply.

Like its parents, a little fox
adapts to its **environment**.
A fox eats rodents, lizards,
insects, and several types
of fruits, but it also likes
to dig through garbage
cans and steal chickens
from farm henhouses.

9

# A Magnificent Fur Coat

The red fox is the most common type of fox. At birth, this fox is covered with beautiful gray fur. Later, a reddish color begins to appear on its head and, little by little, its entire coat takes on a pale copper color. As a pup grows, the pale red becomes darker on its back and head, while the hair on its stomach remains very light. The hair on a fox's cheeks and around its neck is so **dense** that the fox's face looks round.

A fox has a thick tail with a **tapered** white or black tuft at the end. Its belly is covered with short, dense **down**, while its back has longer, colorful hairs. The coat of a red fox is vivid red with a little black in it.

## What do you think?

Why do the coats of foxes change during the year?

**a)** because foxes have winter coats and summer coats

**b)** because their coats get worn out

**c)** because foxes like to wear different colors

The coats of foxes change because the animals have both winter coats and summer coats.

Foxes grow two coats each year. In May, they begin to scratch themselves, and the long, thick hair of their winter coats falls out in large tufts. Foxes look very thin and shabby all summer, but having thinner and shorter hair is the only way they can keep cool in the summer heat. When autumn arrives, and the weather turns colder, they will grow another thick fur coat.

**A little fox holds its pointed ears erect. Its ears can move to catch the smallest sounds. At night, a fox uses its ears and keen sense of smell to find prey.**

**In summer, foxes' coats are short and bristly. Their thin body structure is easier to see when their hair is short.**

The bat-eared fox lives in Africa's **savannas**. With its very large ears, this fox can hear the underground movements of the termites that it likes to eat.

The bottoms of a fox's eyes are lined with a **reflective** layer, like a mirror, that helps the fox see better in the dark. Because a fox takes in plenty of light through its eyes, it is able to hunt at night.

# Out into the World

In autumn, when they are about six months old, young male foxes leave their families. Each must hunt for a new territory of his own, which might include several fields and a woodland. Every day, a fox will roam, or travel, the boundaries of its territory. If a town is nearby, it will usually visit the town's gardens, garages, and garbage cans, too. Curious about everything, a fox is not afraid to approach unfamiliar **dwellings**.

**A fox likes to live alone and near water. It roams the hills, fields, and wooded areas of its territory every day.**

## What do you think?

What do foxes do at night?

a) They gather to play together.

b) They sleep.

c) They climb trees.

At night, foxes gather to play together.

Foxes rest during the day. They take naps in **thickets**,
under the shelter of bushes, or up on tree branches.

When night falls, foxes like to gather in groups to play or groom each other. The groups include foxes that were raised together in the same family. As they meet, the foxes greet each other by swishing their tails and pushing each other with lowered heads. They also **yelp** a hello to each other.

When little foxes from the same family or group meet, they groom each other carefully as a way to show that they recognize one another. They lick each other on the cheeks and chin and nibble at each other's necks and ears.

A fox has more than one way of communicating with other foxes. When it is happy, a fox clucks and yelps softly. When it is frightened or angry, however, a fox growls or barks loudly.

# Mating Season

Near the end of their first year, young foxes have grown quite a bit. They have all now left their dens and moved away from their parents and each other.
Mating season is near, and each young fox will choose a companion so it can begin its own family.
Between December and February, people can hear the nighttime calls of male foxes. The females answer them with high-pitched cries, then the males yelp a response.

When a male fox finds a female companion, he stays with her for about three weeks. They hunt together and mate several times. Their babies will be born in spring.

## What do you think?

Where will a mother fox hide her babies?

a) in a nest

b) in a **burrow**

c) in a ditch

**A mother fox will hide her babies in a burrow.**

Toward the middle of March, a mother fox searches for the place where she will give birth to her babies. The old burrow of a rabbit or a badger is a perfect choice for a fox's den. She digs out the opening a little, then makes the rest of the burrow larger, and places her newborns at ground level. Sometimes, the same burrow will be used by both badgers and foxes. When the different animals need the burrow during the same season, both families mark the entrance and inside with their scents.

A mother fox feeds her babies milk. She does not leave them alone for two or three weeks after they are born, so the pups' father brings her food.

When she is disturbed or senses danger, a mother fox moves her babies, one by one. Carrying them in her mouth by the scruff of their necks, she moves them to the safety of another burrow.

A female fox is an attentive mother. She recognizes her babies by their scent and spends a lot of time grooming them. She calls to her young pups with almost musical cries.

Foxes are mammals, which means they give birth to live babies that drink milk from the mother's body. In the wild, a fox lives about eight years. Foxes live in many regions on Earth — in forests, on mountains, on the plains, and close to areas where humans live. An adult fox weighs between 13 and 27 pounds (6 and 12 kilograms).

Foxes are related to dogs and wolves. The fox family has fourteen different types of foxes.

A fox has long, pointed ears that are held erect on either side of the animal's head.

A fox's tail is bushy and very long, almost as long as the rest of its body. The tail, which is the same color as the fox's coat, is sometimes striped or sprinkled with black hairs and has a white or black tuft of hair at the tip.

From the tip of its nose to the tip of its tail, a fox measures about 4 feet (1.25 meters) long.

From the ground to its withers, or shoulders, a fox measures 13 to 16 inches (33 to 40 centimeters) high.

A fox's mouth is outlined in black.

A fox has thick white markings on the lower half of its face that make the fox look as though it is smiling.

A fox's paws are dark in color and very delicate.

# GLOSSARY

**burrow** — a hole dug in the ground by an animal to be used as its home

**dense** — having parts that are packed closely together

**down** — fine, soft feathers or hair

**dwellings** — houses or shelters

**environment** — the conditions and objects that surround an animal or a human

**erect** — standing straight up

**keen** — sharp or highly sensitive

**moles** — animals with small eyes and long claws that burrow and live underground

**prey** — animals that are hunted and killed by other animals

**reflective** — able to reflect light, images, or sound waves

**savannas** — large, flat areas of grassland with scattered trees, found in warm parts of the world

**shrews** — mouselike animals with long, pointed snouts

**solitary** — being or living alone

**tapered** — gradually becoming narrower or thinner

**territories** — areas of land that animals occupy and defend

**thickets** — dense groups of shrubs or small trees

**venture** — take on the risks and dangers of doing something

**yelp** — make a sharp, high-pitched cry or bark

Please visit our web site at: www.garethstevens.com
For a free color catalog describing Gareth Stevens Publishing's list of high-quality books and multimedia programs, call 1-800-542-2595 (USA) or 1-800-387-3178 (Canada). Gareth Stevens Publishing's fax: (414) 332-3567.

Library of Congress Cataloging-in-Publication Data

Chottin, Ariane.
  [Petit renard. English]
  Little foxes / Ariane Chottin. — North American ed.
    p. cm. — (Born to be wild)
  ISBN 0-8368-4435-1 (lib. bdg.)
  1. Foxes—Infancy—Juvenile literature. I. Title. II. Series.
QL737.C22C555    2005
599.775'139—dc22                    2004057443

This North American edition first published in 2005 by
**Gareth Stevens Publishing**
A WRC Media Company
330 West Olive Street, Suite 100
Milwaukee, Wisconsin 53212 USA

This U.S. edition copyright © 2005 by Gareth Stevens, Inc.
Original edition copyright © 2001 by Mango Jeunesse.

First published in 2001 as *Le petit renard* by Mango Jeunesse, an imprint of Editions Mango, Paris, France.

Picture Credits [t = top, b = bottom, l = left, r = right]
Bios: R. Cavignaux 5, 6; D. Heuclin 7; F. Deschandol 9(t); M. Hill 13(b); F. Cahez 17(t). Colibri: B. Bonnal 4(l); P. Emery 4(b); A. Vuillamy 8; A. M. Loubsens 12(b), 15. Jacana: Varin/Visage 9(b); M. Danegger 12(t), 16, 17(b), 22–23; K. Schneider 20(t). Sunset: FLPA cover; H. Reinhard title page, 3, 19, 22, back cover; Horizon Vision 2; Animals Animals 10; G. Lacz 11, 20(b); N. Dennis 13(t); T. Leeson 18; Alaska Stock 21.

English translation: Pat Lantier
Gareth Stevens editor: Barbara Kiely Miller
Gareth Stevens art direction: Tammy West

Printed in the United States of America

1 2 3 4 5 6 7 8 9 09 08 07 06 05